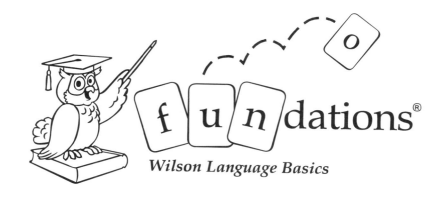

Wilson Language Basics

Student Notebook

Level 3

WILSON

Wilson works.

FIRST EDITION

Wilson Language Training Corporation

www.wilsonlanguage.com

www.fundations.com

Fundations® Student Notebook 3

Item # STNBK3

ISBN 978-1-56778-277-6
FIRST EDITION

PUBLISHED BY:

Wilson Language Training Corporation
47 Old Webster Road
Oxford, MA 01540
United States of America

(800) 899-8454

www.wilsonlanguage.com

Printed in the U.S.A.

November 2007

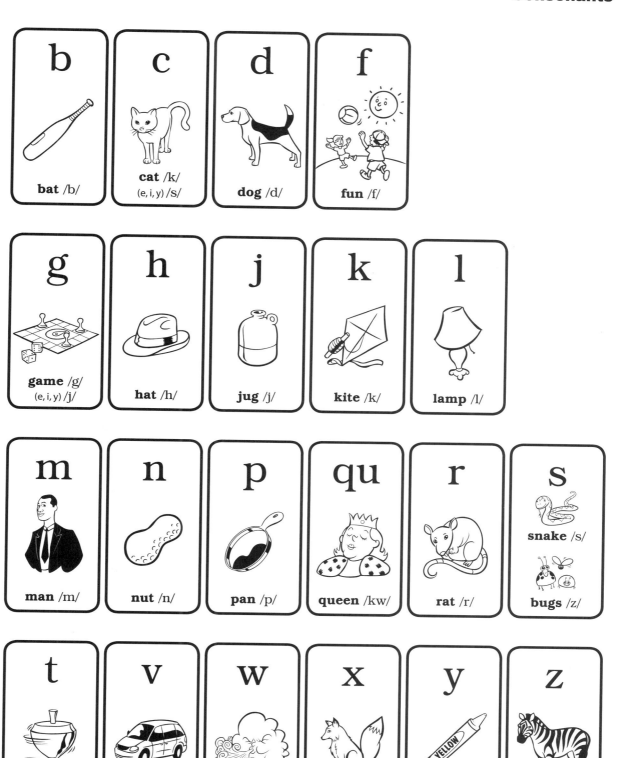

b — **bat** /b/

c — **cat** /k/ (e, i, y) /s/

d — **dog** /d/

f — **fun** /f/

g — **game** /g/ (e, i, y) /j/

h — **hat** /h/

j — **jug** /j/

k — **kite** /k/

l — **lamp** /l/

m — **man** /m/

n — **nut** /n/

p — **pan** /p/

qu — **queen** /kw/

r — **rat** /r/

s — **snake** /s/ / **bugs** /z/

t — **top** /t/

v — **van** /v/

w — **wind** /w/

x — **fox** /ks/

y — **yellow** /y/

z — **zebra** /z/

Digraphs

ch  /ch/

chin

ck  /k/

sock

sh  /sh/

ship

th  /th/

thumb

wh  /w/

whistle

tch	catch	/ch/
dge	fudge	/j/
tion	vacation	/shŭn/
sion	mansion	/shŭn/
sion	television	/zhŭn/
ture	capture	/chər/
tu	spatula	/chü/
ci	glacier	/sh/
ti	patient	/sh/

Silent Letters

wr /r/

wrist

rh /r/

rhyme

gn /n/

gnat

kn /n/

knife

mn /m/

column

mb /m/

lamb

gh /g/

ghost

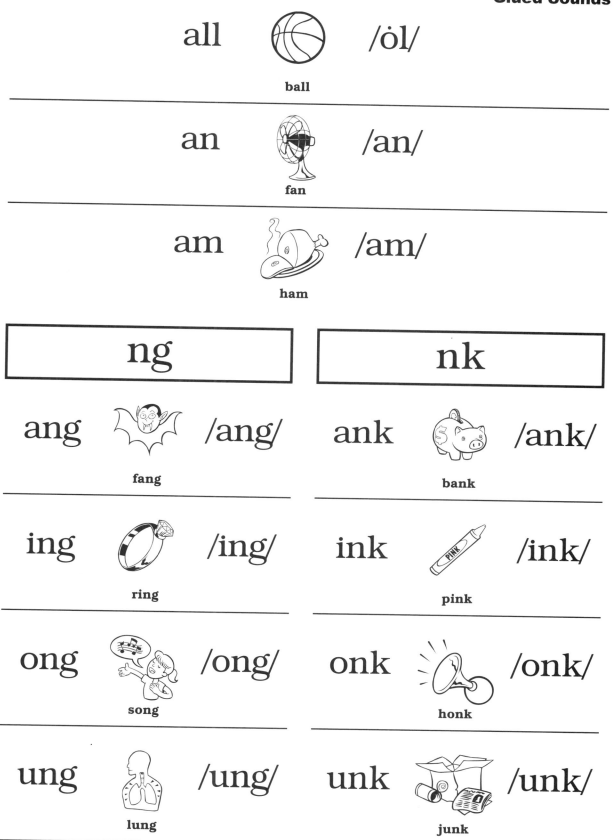

all /öl/

ball

an /an/

fan

am /am/

ham

ng	nk
ang /ang/	ank /ank/
fang	bank
ing /ing/	ink /ink/
ring	pink
ong /ong/	onk /onk/
song	honk
ung /ung/	unk /unk/
lung	junk

Vowels in Closed Syllables

a   /ă/   /ȯ/

apple   wash / squash

e   /ĕ/

Ed

i   /ĭ/

itch

o   /ŏ/

octopus

u   /ŭ/

up

Vowel-Consonant-e

a  /ā/

safe

e  /ē/

Pete

i  /ī/

pine

o  /ō/

home

u  /ū/  /ü/

mule   rule

Vowels In Open Syllables

a   /ā/   /ŭ/

acorn   Alaska

e   /ē/

me

i   /ī/   /ŭ/ or /ĭ/   /ē/

hi   animal   champion

o   /ō/

no

u   /ū/   /ü/

pupil   flu

y   /ī/   /ē/

cry   baby

Vowels

Vowel	Closed Syllable	Vowel-Consonant-e Syllable	Vowel-Open Syllable
a	apple /ă/ wash squash /ȯ/	safe /ā/	acorn /ā/ Alaska /ŭ/
e	Ed /ĕ/	Pete /ē/	me /ē/
i	itch /ĭ/	pine /ī/	hi /ī/ animal /ŭ/ or /ĭ/ champion /ē/
o	octopus /ŏ/	home /ō/	no /ō/
u	up /ŭ/	mule /ū/ rule /ü/	pupil /ū/ flu /ü/
y			cry /ī/ baby /ē/

Closed Syllable Exceptions

ind  /īnd/

find

ild  /īld/

wild

old  /ōld/

cold

olt  /ōlt/

colt

ost  /ōst/

post

Vowel-Consonant-e Exception

ive  /ĭv/

give

R-Controlled Vowels

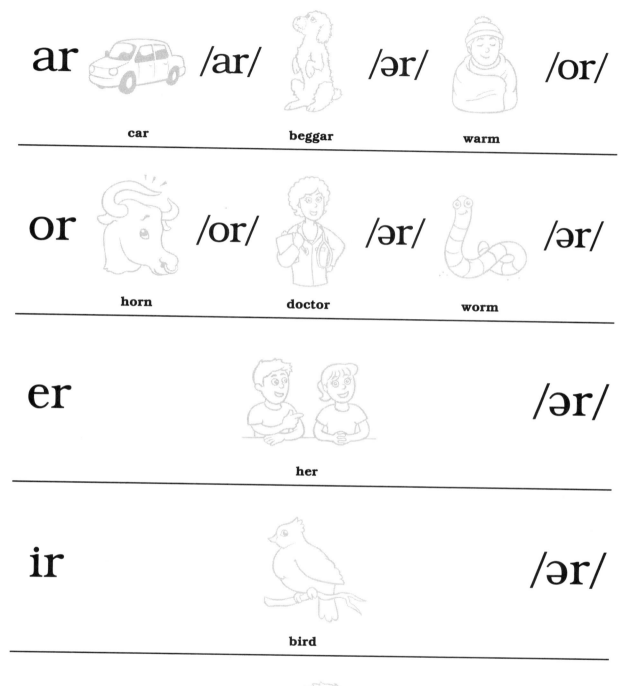

ar /ar/	/ər/	/or/
car	beggar	warm
or /or/	/ər/	/ər/
horn	doctor	worm
er		/ər/
	her	
ir		/ər/
	bird	
ur		/ər/

burn

Vowel Teams

bait
ai

play
ay

eight
eigh

vein
ei

steak
ea

jeep
ee

key
ey

piece
ie

ceiling
ei

eat
ea

bread
ea

light
igh

boat
oa

toe
oe

snow plow
ow

trout soup
ou

suit
ui

blue rescue
ue

chew
ew

school
oo

coin
oi

boy
oy

book
oo

August
au

saw
aw

ai  /ā/

bait

ay  /ā/

play

ee  /ē/

jeep

ea  /ē/

eat

ey  /ē/

key

Vowel Teams

oi  /oi/

coin

oy  /oi/

boy

oa  /ō/

boat

oe  /ō/

toe

ow  /ō/ /ou/

snow   plow

ou 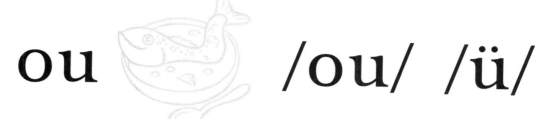 /ou/ /ü/

trout   soup

oo  /ü/

school

ue  /ü/ /ū/

blue   rescue

ew  /ü/

chew

Vowel Teams

au /ȯ/

August

aw /ȯ/

saw

eigh /ā/

eight

ei /ā/

vein

ea /ā/    /ĕ/

steak   bread

ie  /ē/

piece

ei  /ē/

ceiling

igh  /ī/

light

ui  /ü/

suit

oo  /ö/

book

Spelling Options

/w/ →	☐ wind	☐ whistle	
/z/ →	☐ zebra	☐ bugs, wise	
/t/ →	☐ top	☐ jumped	
/s/ →	☐ snake	☐ followed by e, i, y	
/d/ →	☐ dog	☐ thrilled	
/j/ →	☐ jug	☐ followed by e, i, y	
	☐ fudge		
/f/ →	☐ fan	☐ phone	
/k/ →	☐ cat	☐ kite	
	☐ sock	☐ chorus	
/ch/ →	☐ chin	☐ catch	
	☐ spatula /chü/	☐ capture /chər/	

/shŭn/ → ☐ vacation   ☐ mansion

/g/ → ☐ game   ☐ ghost

/r/ → ☐ rat   ☐ wrist

☐ rhyme

/n/ → ☐ nut   ☐ gnat

☐ knife

/m/ → ☐ man   ☐ column

☐ lamb

/sh/ → ☐ ship   ☐ patient

☐ glacier

Spelling Options for Vowel Sounds

/ər/	er	ir	ur	ar	or		

/ā/	a-e	a	ai	ay	eigh	ei	ea

/ē/	e-e	e	y	i	ee	ey	ea	ie	ei

/ī/	i-e	i	y	igh

/ō/	o-e	o	oa	oe	ow

/ū/	u-e	u	ue

/ü/	u-e	u	ue	ew	ou	oo	ui

/oi/	oi	oy

/ou/	ow	ou

/ȯ/	a	au	aw

SYLLABLES

What is a Syllable?

A syllable is a word or part of a word made by **one push of breath**.

A syllable must have a least **one vowel**.

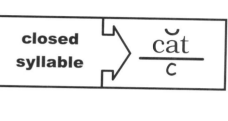

closed syllable

Exception

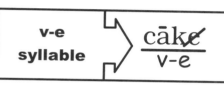

v-e syllable

Exception

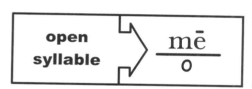

open syllable

Exception

Exception

Exception

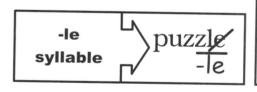

-le syllable

Exception

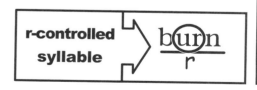

r-controlled syllable

Exception

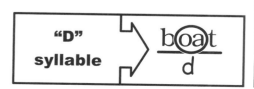

"D" syllable

Exception

Closed Syllables

1. This syllable can only have **one vowel**.

2. The vowel is followed by **one** or **more consonants** (closed in).

3. The vowel sound is **short**. To indicate the short sound, the vowel is marked with a breve (˘).

4. This syllable can be combined with other syllables to make **multisyllabic** words.

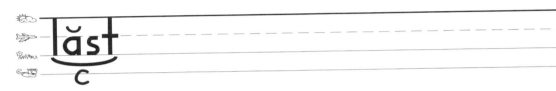

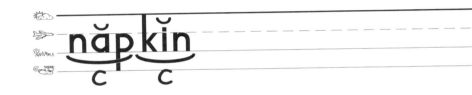

Exceptions: ind, ild, old, olt, ost words

The vowel is usually long even though it is in a closed syllable.

Vowel-Consonant-e Syllables

1. This syllable has a **vowel**, then a **consonant**, then an **e**.

2. The first vowel is **long**. To indicate the long sound, the vowel is marked with a macron (-).

3. The **e** is silent.

4. This syllable can be combined with other syllables to make **multisyllabic** words.

Exceptions: the letter **v**

Sometimes a word has a **vowel**, a **v**, then an **e**. The **e** may make the vowel long (**five**), or it may be there because English words do not end in a **v**. The vowel sound may still be short.

Open Syllables

1. This syllable has only **one vowel** which is the last letter in the syllable.

2. The vowel sound is **long**. To indicate the long sound, the vowel is marked with a macron (ˉ).

3. This syllable can be combined with other syllables to make **multisyllabic** words.

Exceptions: The vowel in an unstressed or unaccented open syllable has a **schwa**. This happens with **a** at the beginning or end of a word.

It happens with **i** in the middle syllable, when the **i** is followed by a **consonant**.

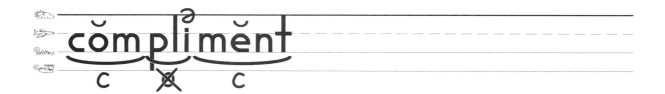

When the **i** is followed by a **vowel**, it often says /ĕ/.

SYLLABLES

Consonant-le Syllables

1. This syllable has only three letters: a **consonant**, an **l**, and an **e**.

2. The **e** is silent. It is the vowel. Every syllable needs at least one vowel. The consonant and the l are sounded like a blend.

3. This syllable must be the last syllable in a **multisyllabic** word.

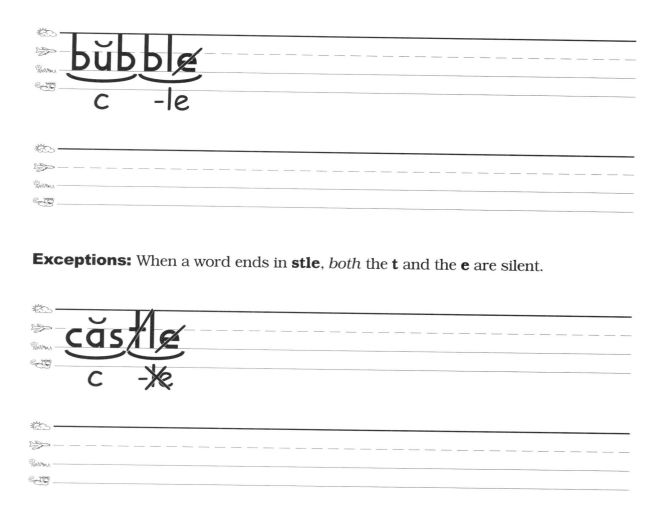

Exceptions: When a word ends in **stle**, *both* the **t** and the **e** are silent.

R-Controlled Syllables

1. This syllable contains a single vowel followed by an **r** (**ar, er, ir, or, ur**).

2. The vowel is neither **long** nor **short**; it is controlled by the **r**.

3. This syllable can be combined with other syllables to make **multisyllabic** words.

Exceptions: rr

When a vowel is followed by a double **r** (**rr**), the vowel before it might have a short sound.

Vowel Digraph / Diphthong ("D" Syllables)

1. This syllable contains a **vowel digraph** or a **diphthong**. These are vowel teams.

Vowel Digraph:
Two vowels together that represent one sound (**ee**)

Diphthong:
A sound that begins with one vowel sound and glides into another (**oi**)

Exceptions: Sometimes two vowels together do not form a vowel team. The two vowels are split and the word is divided into syllables between the two vowels.

Four Ways to spell /k/

ck sock /k/

Use **ck** at the end of a one syllable word, right after the vowel.

Use **ck** in compound words.

so<u>ck</u>

pi<u>ck</u>

humpba<u>ck</u>

c /k/

Use **c** at the beginning of most words.

Use **c** in a blend at the beginning of a word.

Use **c** in multisyllabic words ending with **ic**.

<u>c</u>at

<u>c</u>rash

picni<u>c</u>

k /k/

Use **k** in glued sounds with **nk**.

Use **k** in blends at the end of a word.

Use **k** in vowel-consonant-e words.

p<u>ink</u>

mil<u>k</u>

bi<u>k</u>e

ch /k/

Use **ch** at the beginning of some words and with some /**sk**/ blends.

<u>ch</u>orus

s<u>ch</u>ool

Spelling with ck and tch

Spelling with ck

At the end of a one syllable word, use **ck** right after a short vowel. After a consonant, use **k**.

Words with k   **Words with ck**

Spelling with tch

At the end of a one syllable word, use **tch** right after a short vowel. After a consonant, use **ch**.

Words with ch   **Words with tch**

Spelling Words with schwa

 ## In Closed Syllables

In words with unaccented closed syllables, the unaccented vowel sound might be spelled with any vowel. Use sound option spelling.

In words with unaccented closed syllables ending in **n**, the **schwa** is usually spelled with an **o** or an **e**.

In words with unaccented closed syllables ending in **/ĭt/**, the **schwa** is usually spelled with an **et**.

The Baseword/Suffix Rules

Baseword

A **baseword** is a word that can stand alone as a word or have something added to it.

Suffix

A **suffix** is an ending that can be added to a baseword.

Plurals

A **plural** word is a word that means more than one thing.

Most nouns add **s** to make them plural.

_____   _____
_____   _____
_____   _____
_____   _____

Nouns ending in **s**, **x**, **z**, **ch**, **tch** and **sh** add **es**.

_____   _____
_____   _____
_____   _____
_____   _____

_____   _____
_____   _____
_____   _____
_____   _____

SPELLING

The 1-1-1 Doubling Rule

 Doubling Words

1-1-1 words are closed or r-controlled words with 1 syllable, 1 vowel, and 1 consonant after the vowel.

Example: ship + ing = shipping

When adding a vowel suffix to a 1-1-1 doubling baseword, double the final consonant.

cup + ed =

flat + est =

star + ing =

When adding a consonant suffix to a 1-1-1 doubling baseword, just add the suffix.

cup + ful =

flat + ly =

ship + ment =

The consonants **h**, **j**, **k**, **v**, **w**, **x**, **y** and **z** do not double in English words.

The Silent e and Suffix Rule

 ## Adding a Suffix

When adding a vowel suffix to a baseword ending in **e**, drop the **e**.

glide + ing =

dance + er =

live + ing =

juggle + ing =

When adding a consonant suffix to a baseword ending in **e**, just add the suffix.

like + ly =

life + less =

This rule also applies to words ending in a consonant -le syllable.

settle + ing =

settle + ment =

SPELLING

The y and Suffix Rule

 ## Following a Consonant

If **y** follows a consonant in an open syllable, change **y** to **i** when adding *any* suffix. The **i** retains the original sound of the **y**.

cry + ed =

empty + ed =

cry + s =

empty + ness =

 ## Suffix Plus Suffix

If the **y** suffix is added to a baseword and then another suffix is added, change the **y** suffix to **i** and add the other suffix.

Example: dirt + y = dirty   dirty + est = dirtiest

dirty + est =

lonely + ness =

Exception: When the suffix begins with **i**, do not change the **y** to **i**, just add the suffix.

baby + ish =

The y and Suffix Rule (continued)

 Forming Plurals

When forming plurals, change **y** to **i** and add **es**. The **-es** suffix says /**z**/.

Example: baby = babies

penny =

lady =

 D Syllable

If **y** is part of a dipthong or vowel digraph ("D" Syllable), just add the suffix.

play + ed =

volley + ing =

play + ful =

employ + ment =

Making Contractions

1. Identify the two words you are putting together.

2. Take letters away from the 2nd word - **never the first**! Put the apostrophe in the place of the missing letters.

When Contracting:	Take Away:
not	o
is	i
will	wi
are	a
would	woul
have	ha

is not = _____

there is = _____

they will = _____

we are = _____

I would = _____

you have = _____

Special cases:

must not = mustn't   let us = let's

will not = won't   I am = I'm

do not = don't

can not = can't

es

ing

ed /əd/

ed /d/

ed /t/

er

est

ish

able

en

ive

y

Vowel Suffixes

al   ent

an   or

ous

Wilson Fundations | ©2005 Wilson Language Training Corporation

s

ful

ment

ness

less

ly

ty

ward

SPELLING

Spelling Options

A	B	C
absent	bake	cake
ape	basket	came
	bike	cane
	bite	care
	blaze	cave
	bone	choke
	Boston	chose
	bucket	close
		cone
		confuse
		craze
		cricket
		cube

D

dare
denim
dime
dive
doze
dragon
drive

F

falcon
file
fire
flame
flute
froze
fuse

G

globe
grade
grape
graze

_____

_____

_____

_____

_____

_____

_____

_____

_____

Spelling Options

H	J	K
haze	jacket	kite
helmet	jackets	
helmets	joke	
hide		
hole		
home		
hope		

SPELLING

L

lake
lane
lemon
like
lime
line
locket

M

magnet
magnets
maze
maze
melon
mile
mine
mule

N

name
nine
nose
note

SPELLING

SPELLING

O
oxen

P
packet
pile
plane
planet
planets
plate
pocket
poke
pole
pose
pretzel
problem
prune

Qu
quake

R

racket
ride
ripe
rocket
rockets
rope
rose
rule

S

salad
sale
scrape
seven
share
shine
slide
slope
smile
snake
spine
spoke
state

T

talent
tape
Texas
these
those
throne
ticket
tide
tonsil
trade
travel
trumpet
tube
tune

SPELLING

Spelling Options

U	V	W
use	velvet	wagon
	vote	wave
		whale
		whine
		white
		wide
		wife
		wine
		wipe

Aa

Aa

Aa

Vocabulary

Aa

Aa

Bb

Wilson Fundations | ©2005 Wilson Language Training Corporation

ABCDEF

Bb

Cc

Cc

ABCDEF

Vocabulary

C c

Wilson Fundations | ©2005 Wilson Language Training Corporation

Cc

Cc

Cc

Vocabulary

Cc

Cc

Dd

ABCDEF

Dd

Dd

Dd

ABCDEF

Vocabulary

Ee

Ff

Gg

Wilson Fundations | ©2005 Wilson Language Training Corporation

Hh

Hh

Hh

GHIJKL

Vocabulary

Hh

Hh

Ii

Ii

Kk

Ll

GHIJKL

Vocabulary

Mm

Mm

Mm

Oo

Pp

Pp

MNOPQuRS

Vocabulary

Pp

Rr

Rr

M N O P Qu R S

Rr

Ss

Ss

M N O P Qu R S

Vocabulary

Ss

Ss

Ss

M N O P Qu R S

S s

S s

S s

MNOPQuRS

Vocabulary

S s

S s

S s

MNOPQuRS

Ss

Ss

Ss

M N O P Qu R S

T t

T t

V v

TUVWXYZ

W w

W w

W w

Trick Words

A
again
also
America
animal
another
answer
any
are
August
away

B
beautiful
because
been
before
being
bought
breakfast
brother
build

C
carry
change
city
color
come
could
country
cousin

_____

_____

_____

_____

_____

_____

_____

_____

D

dance
daughter
December
different
does

E

early
earth
enough
even
every
example
eye

F

family
favorite
February
friend
from

Trick Words

G
great

H
have
head
here
house

J
January
July

L
laugh
learn
library
lose

M
many
Monday
month
more
mother
move
Mr.
Mrs.

N
neighbor
none
nothing

_____

_____

_____

_____

_____

_____

_____

_____

O

ocean
often
only
other
our

P

paste
people
picture
piece
place
put

R

ready

M N O P Qu R S

S

said
Saturday
says
school
should
something
special
strange
sugar

T

they
thought
Thursday
together
too
trouble
Tuesday

U

use
used

TUVWXYZ

Trick Words

V	W	Y
very	want	years
	was	young
	water	your
	Wednesday	
	were	
	what	
	when	
	who	
	why	
	words	
	work	
	world	

A
ate
eight

_____

_____

_____

_____

B
band
banned

_____

_____

_____

banned
band

_____

_____

_____

berry
bury

_____

_____

_____

_____

Sound Alikes

B

brake
break

_____

_____

_____

break
brake

_____

_____

_____

bury
berry

_____

_____

_____

B

buy
by, bye

_____

_____

_____

by
buy, bye

_____

_____

_____

bye
buy, by

_____

_____

_____

C
cell
sell

_____

_____

_____

cent
scent, sent

_____

_____

_____

E
eight
ate

_____

_____

_____

Sound Alikes

F
farther
father

_____

_____

_____

father
farther

_____

_____

_____

find
fined

_____

_____

_____

F
fined
find

_____

_____

_____

flour
flower

_____

_____

_____

flower
flour

_____

_____

_____

G
guessed
guest

_____

_____

_____

guest
guessed

_____

_____

_____

H
heard
herd

_____

_____

_____

herd
heard

_____

_____

_____

hi
high

_____

_____

_____

H

high
hi

_____

_____

_____

I

its
it's

_____

_____

_____

it's
its

_____

_____

_____

K

knew
new

_____

_____

_____

knight
night

_____

_____

_____

know
no

_____

_____

_____

K

knows
nose

_____

_____

_____

L
lead
led

_____

_____

_____

led
lead

_____

_____

_____

M
mail
male

_____

_____

_____

male
mail

_____

_____

_____

meat
meet

_____

_____

_____

M N O P Qu R S

M

meet
meat

_____

_____

_____

M

missed
mist

_____

_____

_____

mind
mined

_____

_____

_____

mist
missed

_____

_____

_____

mined
mind

_____

_____

_____

M N O P Qu R S

N
new
knew

_____

_____

_____

_____

night
knight

_____

_____

_____

_____

no
know

_____

_____

_____

N
nose
knows

_____

_____

_____

O
oh
owe

_____

_____

_____

owe
oh

_____

_____

_____

P
pail
pale

_____

_____

_____

pale
pail

_____

_____

_____

peace
piece

_____

_____

_____

MNOPQuRS

P

piece
peace

_____

_____

_____

_____

P

principal
principle

_____

_____

_____

_____

plain
plane

_____

_____

_____

_____

principle
principal

_____

_____

_____

_____

plane
plain

_____

_____

_____

_____

R
right
write

_____

_____

_____

S
sail
sale

_____

_____

_____

sale
sail

_____

_____

_____

scene
seen

_____

_____

_____

MNOPQuRS

S

scent
cent, sent

_____

_____

_____

seen
scene

_____

_____

_____

sell
cell

_____

_____

_____

S

sent
cent, scent

_____

_____

_____

side
sighed

_____

_____

_____

sighed
side

_____

_____

_____

S

some
sum

_____

_____

_____

son
sun

_____

_____

_____

stationary
stationery

_____

_____

_____

S

stationery
stationary

_____

_____

_____

straight
strait

_____

_____

_____

strait
straight

_____

_____

_____

MNOPQuRS

S

sum
some

_____

_____

_____

_____

sun
son

_____

_____

_____

_____

T

their
there, they're

_____

_____

_____

_____

there
their, they're

_____

_____

_____

_____

they're
their, there

_____

_____

_____

_____

TUVWXYZ

T

throne
thrown

_____

_____

_____

thrown
throne

_____

_____

_____

W

wait
weight

_____

_____

_____

warn
worn

_____

_____

_____

weak
week

_____

_____

_____

TUVWXYZ

TUVWXYZ

$\mathbb{W}$

wear
where

_____

_____

_____

_____

$\mathbb{W}$

weight
wait

_____

_____

_____

_____

weather
whether

_____

_____

_____

_____

where
wear

_____

_____

_____

_____

week
weak

_____

_____

_____

_____

whether
weather

_____

_____

_____

_____

W

which
witch

_____

_____

_____

_____

witch
which

_____

_____

_____

_____

worn
warn

_____

_____

_____

_____

W

write
right

_____

_____

_____

_____

TUVWXYZ

NOTES